My Feelings Journal

Copyright Christina Dreve

All Rights Reserved

First Printing 2017

Second Printing 2021

ISBN 978-1-952665-86-8

Copper Canopy Press

www.coppercanopypress.com

Cover Art by Jack Archer https://www.facebook.com/groups/275622803442332/

Hand Drawn Fonts by Grace Hayden

My Feelings Journal:

Writing Prompts With Over

2100 Emotion Words

Christina Dreve

Dedication

For You;

that you may feel present in your body

and know

you are perfect

exactly as you are

right now.

Contents

How to Use This book	4
Emotion Words	6
Guided Exercises	
Cycle One	41
Cycle Two	51
Cycle Three	61
Cycle Four	71
Cycle Five	81
Cycle Six	91
Cycle Seven	101
Afterword	111
About the Author	113

How to Use this Book

When you practice noticing what's inside your head you can begin a conversation with yourself. Experiencing emotion is one of the ways our body communicates with our intellect.

Setting aside self-judgment will connect you to your feelings more easily. As you practice accepting your feelings (without shaming or criticizing yourself) you'll grow in self-confidence and awareness. Sometimes our feelings get our attention before it registers as a thought. Being more aware will improve the conversations you have with yourself because those are the most important conversations you can have.

You may use this book every day, or only when things feel out of balance. Your first priority is always your physical safety. Once you know there are no threats to your well-being, you may find that feeling poorly (and feeling great) comes from what you tell yourself.

When you understand emotions create hormones and those are what create thoughts, coping with feeling those feelings is easier. It's also freeing to know that you don't have to act upon those feelings.

Here's a quick way to connect in to your body... close your eyes and take a deep breath while counting to four. Notice how your belly fills up as you inhale, pause for a moment, then let your shoulders relax as you exhale to the count of four. Breathe deeply with your eyes closed, then move your attention to your toes. Think about how they balance your steps, and move you in the direction you want to go. See if you can feel any emotions there, and continue to mentally move your attention up through your legs... pause as you consider each part of you, and let your body tell you whatever it needs to.

This may seem strange since we don't often talk directly to ourselves, but there is wisdom that lives inside of every part of us. Truly taking care of yourself means that you understand what you're thinking and feeling, and that you're paying attention to the wisdom of your body.

Knowing your true opinion and understanding where that comes from creates incredible confidence. When you can detach from your thoughts and see them as a story you tell yourself in attempt to control what happens next time, you empower yourself.

Based on the research of brain scientist Jill Bolte Taylor, staying present with a feeling for 90 seconds allows your body to process your brain's hormone release. While it can be uncomfortable in the moment, being aware of the science of the chemical flow helps me stay with it.

The challenge here is not to be the boss of your body and tell it what to do, but to simply watch how it works. If you can transition from having an opinion on the state of your clothing size to letting your body tell you what it needs, you'll find out how you really feel. Your body will know it's safe to communicate with your mind. This is a bold claim, but your intuition will strengthen through this practice, and you'll trust yourself more.

As you continue to move your attention through your body, think about how every part of you works together as one unit. Listen for words that pop into your head, be aware of colors you see behind your eyelids, and relax your judging of every part of your body. Act as though you are observing an artist's painting for color balance and overall mood. Let the painting that is your body speak for itself without your intellectual opinion talking over it.

This process of connecting to your feelings works best when you notice without judging yourself. It takes practice to fully listen to what your body needs to tell you. As you practice accepting your feelings without shaming or criticizing yourself, you benefit even more. Try to allow your body the freedom to speak without fear of criticism. Use these sentence starters to talk to all the parts of yourself, and then simply fill in the blank. Write whatever you need to, because this book is for your eyes only.

This journal gives you week-by-week pages to fill in over one month's time. Of course you may use more than one each day, or only one a week. This is your journal, so let it work for you.

Ready? Let's begin!

Emotion Words

Use this list to match words to your body's message. Feel free to make up new feelings, combine words as needed, and add descriptions in the spaces and margins. Give yourself full permission to explore your ideas since there's no way to get this wrong. Breathe deeply and follow what interests you in the moment. You can also flip through the emotion words, close your eyes, and place your finger somewhere on the page. Open your eyes and write how you may or may not relate to that description. The guided exercises follow the emotion words to record anything you notice.

<u>A</u>

abraded

abrasive

absent

absent minded

absorbed

abused

acceptance

accepting

accomplished

accountable

aching

acting

adamant

admiration

adoration

advanced

adventurous

advocate

affection

affectionate

afflicted

afraid

against the grain

aged

ageless

aggravated

aggressive

agitated

agitation

agonized

agony

airtight

airy

alarmed

alert

alienated	anguished	armed
alienation	angular	armored
aligned	animated	arousal
alive	animosity	aroused
all encompassing	annoyed	arrogant
all knowing	anointed	artificial
all seeing	anticipating	ascended
aloof	antiseptic	asexual
amazed	antisocial	ashamed
amazement	anxiety filled	aspiring
ambiguous	anxious	assaulted
ambivalent	apathetic	assembled
ambling	apeish	assertive
amended	apologetic	assured
amending	appalled	astonished
amiable	appearing	astonishment
amnesia	appreciative	asymmetrical
amputated	apprehensive	at arms
amused	appropriate	at fault
amusement	ardent	atonal
anesthetized	ardor	attachment
anger	argumentative	attacked
angry	arid	attention seeking

attracted	**B**	bedazzled
attraction	backsliding	befuddled
attractive	backwards	bejeweled
attuned	bad	beleaguered
augmented	baffled	belief
automated	bald	bemused
automatic	balding	benched
aversion	banished	bent
avoidant	bankrupt	bereaved
awarded	banshee	betrayed
aware	baptized	bewildered
awe	bare naked	bewitched
awe filled	barking	biased
awed	barred	big hearted
awesome	barren	bigfoot
awestruck	barrier	bitter
awful	base	black
awkward	baseless	black cat
	bashful	bland
	batty	bleached
	bearded	bleary
	beat	bleary eyed
	beaten	bleeding

blended	born again	bright
blending	bought	brittle
blessed	bound	broke
blessing	bounty	broken
blind	bounty price	brown
blinded	bowled over	brownie
blindsided	braced	bubbly
bliss	bracing	bullish
blissful	braggadocios	bumpy
blistered	brainwashed	buoyant
bloated	braked	buoyed
blown	brakes locked	burdened
blue	branded	burned out
blurred	brandied	bursting
blurry	brassy	businesslike
bodacious	brave	butch
boiling	breaking	buttery
boiling over	breaking apart	
bold	breathless	
bookish	breathy	
boomeranged	breezy	
bored	bride like	
boredom	bride price	

C

calculating
called
called out
calloused
calm
camouflaged
canopied
capricious
captain
captivated
captive
captured
carefree
caregiver
careless
caretaking
caring
castrated
cat and mouse
cat like
catty
caustic
cauterized
cautious
celebrated
cell
cellular
centaur
centered
certain
chagrined
challenged
changed
changeling
changing
chaos
chaotic
charged
charred
chased
chasing
chattel
chatty
cheated
chewy
chiding
chimera
chiming
chipped
chivalrous
choice
choked
choking
choosy
chortling
chosen
circling
civilized
clean
clear
clear headed
clever
cliquish
clocked
close
close mouthed
closed
closed off

closeness	complete	coppered
closeted	compliant	coppery
cloudy	comradery	cornered
coachable	condemned	corporal
cobalt	confident	correct
cocked	conflicted	costumed
cohesive	confused	courageous
cold	connected	covered
collapsed	connection	covered up
collapsing	conscious	coveting
collected	considerate	covetousness
colorful	consideration	crabby
comfortable	conspiring	cracked
comforted	contained	cranky
coming apart	contempt	craving
commandeered	content	crazed
committed	contentment	crazy
community	contracted	creating
companion	contrary	creative
compartmentalized	controlled	creativity
compassion	cooperation	crinkly
compassionate	cooperative	cross
complacent	copper	crouched

crouching	**D**	dehydrated
crowded	dammed up	dejected
crumbling	damned	delaminated
crunchy	dancing	delicate
crushed	daring	delighted
crusty	dark	delivered
crying	dazed	demanding
culpable	dazzled	demon
cultivated	dead	dependent
cultured	debonair	dependence
curious	deceived	dependent
curled	declassified	depleted
cursed	declining	deported
cussed	decomposing	deposed
cut off	defeated	depressed
cyclops	defeminized	deprived
	defenseless	deserted
	defiance	despair
	defiant	despairing
	defined	despondent
	deflated	destroyer
	deformed	detached
	degraded	determined

devastated	disbelieving	disoriented
developed	disbursed	disparaging
developing	disciplined	displaced
devising	discombobulated	displeased
devote	disconcerted	disquiet
devoted	disconnected	disquieted
devotion	discontent	disreputable
devoured	discontented	distanced
devourer	discordant	distant
difficult	discouraged	distaste
dimensional	disenchanted	distracted
diminutive	disgruntled	distracting
dimpled	disguised	distraction
dimwitted	disgust	distraught
diplomatic	disgusted	distress
dire	disheartened	distressed
dirty	disillusioned	distrustful
disabled	disintegrating	disturbed
disappointed	disinterested	dizzy
disarmed	dislike	doe eyed
disassembled	disliked	dog eared
disbanded	dislocated	dolce
disbelief	dismayed	dominating

domineering	dull	**E**
done for	dumbstruck	eager
doomed	duped	eagerness
dopey	dusty	earnest
doting	dwarfed	earthing
doubtful	dying	earthling
downcast	dynamic	earthly
dragon	dysphoric	earthy
drained		easy
drawn toward		easy going
dread		ebbing
dreaming		ebullient
dreamy		ecstasy
dried out		ecstatic
dripping		edgy
drive		educated
drooped		effluviant
drooping		elated
drought		elation
drowning		elected
drunk		eliminated
dry		elongated
due		elysian

emancipated	energetic	excited
emasculated	engaged	exciting
embarrassed	engrossed	excluded
emblazoned	enjoy	exclusive
emboldened	enjoying	excused
embraced	enjoyment	excusing
embroiled	enlivened	exhausted
emerged	enraged	exhilarated
emergent	enraptured	expansive
emerging	entangled	expectant
empathetic	enthralled	expired
empathic	enthusiastic	exploited
empowered	entitled	exploitive
empty	entranced	explosive
enabled	envious	exposed
enabler	envy	extroverted
encapsulated	escaped	exuberant
enchanted	eternal	
enclosed	ethereal	
encompassing	ethers	
encouraged	evil	
encumbered	exasperated	
ending	exasperation	

F

faded	fatigued	flanked
fading	favored	flaring
faint	fay	flat
fair	fear	flatulent
fairness	fearful	fleeing
fairylike	fearless	flexible
faith filled	fed	flimsy
faithful	feeling	floating
faithless	feminine	flooded
fake	fermented	flowery
faking	fervor	flowing
fakir	fictional	fluffed
fallen	fidgety	fluffy
falling	fiery	fluid
falling apart	fight or flight	flustered
famished	fileted	flux
famous	filled	flying
fancy	filmy	foamy
fascinated	fire tested	focused
fascination	fireproof	foiled
fatalistic	firm	folded
fatigue	fishy	fond
	flaky	fondness

fool hardy	freaked out	funny
fooled	freaky	furious
foolish	free	furrowed
forbidden	freed	furtive
forced	freedom	fury
forceful	fresh	
foreboding	fretful	
foreign	fretting	
forgetful	friendship	
forgiven	fright	
forgiving	frightened	
forgotten	frightful	
forked	frisky	
forlorn	frost proof	
formal	frosty	
formed	frustrated	
formless	fugitive	
forsaken	fulfilled	
fractured	full	
fragile	full of holes	
fraught	fuming	
frayed	fun	
frazzled	funereal	

G

galvanized	glowing	grief-stricken
gamey	gluttonous	grim
gaudy	gluttony	gritty
gay	goblin	grizzly
gelatinous	god fearing	grouchy
gelded	god like	ground down
general	golden	grounded
generating	golem	growing
generative	gong	growling
generous	gonging	grueling
genius	grabbed	gruesome
genocidal	grabbing	grumbling
gentile	grace	grumpy
gently	graceful	guarded
ghost like	gracious	guardian
ghoul	grateful	guided
giddy	gray	guilt
gifted	greasy	guilty
gilded	greed	gummy
glad	greedy	gurgling
gloating	green	gutless
gloomy	gremlin	gypsy
	grief	

H

- hack
- hacked
- hag
- haggard
- haggardly
- haha
- haiku
- hail
- hailed
- hallowed
- hallucinating
- haloed
- hammered
- hankering
- happiness
- happy
- harangued
- hard
- hardy
- hard pressed
- hardened
- harmed
- harmonic
- harmonious
- harmonized
- harmonizing
- harnessed
- harrowed
- harsh
- hate
- hateful
- headstrong
- healed
- healer
- healing
- healthy
- hearing
- heart torn out
- heartbroken
- heavily burdened
- heavy
- heavy hearted
- hefty
- held
- hell bent
- hellion
- helpful
- helpless
- heralded
- herbed
- heroic
- hesitant
- hewn
- hidden
- hilarious
- hip
- hitched
- hitchhiker
- hoarse
- hobgoblin
- holy
- homogenous
- honest
- hoodwinked
- hope
- hopeful
- hopeless
- horned

horny	**I**	inadequate
horrified	icy	inappropriate
horror	ideal	inauthentic
hostile	idealize	incensed
hounded	ignorant	inciting
howling	ignored	included
hugged	ignoring	inclusion
human	ill mannered	inclusive
humiliated	illusions	incoherent
humorous	imagining	inconsolable
hung out	impassioned	incorporated
hungry	impatient	incredulous
hunted	impish	indecisive
hurled	impulsive	indifferent
hurried	in a rut	indignant
hurt	in awe	indigo
hurtful	in pieces	inebriated
hurting	in service	infantilized
husky	in the wrong	infatuated
hyper	in the wrong era	inferior
hyper drive	in the zone	inflamed
hysteria	in tune	informal
hysterical	inactive	infrequent

infuriated	introspective	**J**
ingrained	introverted	jaded
ingrown	intuitive	jailed
inhuman	invertebrate	jammed
initiative	invested	jealous
injured	invigorated	jittery
inner knowing	invisible	joking
innovative	involved	jolly
insecure	irate	jovial
insecurity	irked	joy
insensitive	irritable	joyful
inspired	irritated	joyous
insubordinate	isolated	jubilant
insulting		judgmental
integrated		juggling
intent		jumpy
intercessor		jury rigged
interested		just
interior		justice
interrogated		jutting
intimidated		
intoxicated		
intrigued		

K

keen
kelpie
kept
kicked
kind
kindhearted
kingly
kissed
knocked around
knotted
knowledgeable
koan

L

labeled
laid back
lauded
laughing
laughter
lawless
layered
lazy
leader
leafy
learned
learning
lecherous
lechery
leech
leery
lenient
leprechaun
let down
lethargic
level
level headed

levelled
liberated
libido
lifeless
lighted
liked
liking
limited
limp
lion hearted
lioness
listening
listless
lit
lit up
lively
livid
living
loaded
loathing
lonely
longing
loose

loss	**M**	meeting
lost	mad	melancholy
loud	made up	melded
love	magical	mellow
loveable	magnanimous	melodious
loved	magnetic	melted
lovely	magnified	memorable
loving	major	memorial
low	maligned	memorialized
lowing	malleable	mended
lulled	mangy	merged
lumpy	mania	mermaid
lust	manly	messed with
	marching	met
	masculine	metal
	matriarch	metallic
	matriarchal	mild
	maudlin	mildewed
	mean	milky
	mechanical	minimal
	medusa	minimalized
	meek	minimized
	meet	minotaur

minted	molten	mutant
misaligned	moody	mutilated
misappropriated	mooing	mystified
mischievous	moony	
misdirected	mortal	
miserable	mortification	
misery	mortified	
misfit	moth eaten	
misgiving	moth man	
misguided	mottled	
misled	mourned	
misrepresented	mourning	
missed	mousy	
misshapen	moved	
missile	movement	
mistaken	moving	
mistrustful	moxie	
misty	moxy	
misunderstood	multidimensional	
mixed up	murderous	
modest	murky	
molded	muse	
moldy	mushy	

N

naked
named
nameless
naughty
near sighted
needed
neglected
neglectful
nerdy
nervous
neutral
new
newly minted
nightmarish
nimble
nirvana
no brakes
nonchalant
noncommittal
nostalgic
noticeable
noticed

nourished
nubby
numb
nurtured
nurturing
nutty
nymph

O

oaky
obdurate
obedient
obligated
obliged
obliterated
obscure
obscured
obsolete
obstinate
offended
offensive
ogre
oily
old
old fashioned
omnipresent
omniscient
opaque
open
open hearted
optimistic

orange	**P**	partnership
ordered	pain	passageway
ornery	pained	passed
out of breath	painful	passenger
out of control	painless	passing
out of place	panic	passion
out of step	panicked	passionate
outcast	papery	passive
outclassed	paralyzed	pathetic
outed	parched	pathological
outmoded	pardoned	patience
outnumbered	pared	patient
outrage	pared down	patina
outraged	parented	patrial
outside	pariah	patriarch
outsider	parked	patriarchal
overcooked	part	patrician
overjoyed	parted	patrol
overwhelmed	particle	patrolled
overwrought	particular	patron
oxidized	parting	patronal
	partner	patronized
	partnered	patronizing

paving	periwinkle	pining
paw	perk	pink
pawn	perked	pinned
pax	perky	pious
peace	permanent	pissed
peaceful	permitted	pitied
peacemaker	perplexed	pity
peckish	persecuted	pivoting
pedestrian	persevering	plain
peeled	persnickety	planted
peeled back	persuasive	planted
peeling	perturbed	plastic
pegasus	perverse	platinum
pent up	pessimism	play
perfect	pessimistic	playacting
perfection	petrified	playful
perfectionist	phobic	playing
perfector	phoenix	pleased
perform	picked	plentiful
performing	pickled	poetic
perfunctory	picturing	pointed
periodic	pieced together	pointy
perishing	pinched	poisonous

policed	prickly	protected
polished	pride	proud
poorly behaved	prideful	provocateur
popular	prideless	provocative
positive	primed	provoked
poufy	princely	prowling
power	privacy	prudent
powerful	private	prudish
powerless	privileged	pruned
pragmatic	proactive	psychic
prayerful	proclivity	puckered
precious	prodigal	puffy
predatory	prodigal son	pulled
predilection	prodigious	punched
preferential	producing	puny
preferred	productive	puppy like
preoccupied	professional	purple
prepared	progressive	pursued
pressed	prolific	push
pressured	promoted	pushy
pretending	propensity	putrid
pretentious	prophetic	puzzled
prevented	prosecuted	

Q	R	
quacking	rabid	rebellious
quaked	racist	rebounded
quaking	radiant	rebounding
qualified	rage	rebuilt
quarrelsome	rageful	recalcitrant
quelched	ragged	recalled
querulous	ragged edged	received
questioned	raging	receiving
questioning	rakish	receptive
quiet	rambling	reclaimed
quieted	rank and file	recovered
	raped	recovering
	rapid	recovery
	rapture	red
	rapturous	reddened
	rational	redeemed
	rationalize	redirected
	rationalizing	reestablished
	rattled	reflective
	ready	refreshed
	rebel	refugee
	rebelling	refused
		refusing

regenerated	repelled	retrofitted
regretful	repentant	returned
regurgitated	reprehensible	revenge filled
rehabbed	representative	revengeful
rehabilitating	repulsed	reversed
reincarnated	reputable	revising
reinforced	required	revived
rejected	resentful	revulsed
rejuvenated	reserved	revulsion
relaxation	resigned	rewarded
relaxed	resolute	ribald
release	resolved	riddle
released	resonant	rigged
reliable	resounding	rigged
relieved	respect	right
relish	respectful	righteous
remade	responsible	riot ready
remorse	rested	riotous
remorseful	restful	robbed
removed	restless	robotic
renewed	restored	rock 'n roll
repaired	restrained	rolled over
repellant	retrained	rolling

rookish	**S**	schmaltzy
roomy	sad	scorned
rooted	sadness	screwed
rotten	safe	screwed over
rough hewn	salivating	secret
round	salty	secretive
rounded	salvaged	secure
roused	same	see through
routed	sappy	seeing
royal	sarcastic	seeking
rude	sardonic	seething
rugged	satisfaction	segmented
ruin	satisfied	selected
ruination	satyr	self conscious
run	saved	self doubt
run out	savory	self loathing
running	scalded	self reliant
running away	scandalized	self sufficient
rusted	scared	selfish
rutted	scarred	selfless
	scary	sensitive
	scattered	sensitivity
	scheduled	septic

serene	short	sinking
serenity	short circuited	sipping
settled	short sighted	siren
sexual	shredded	sitting
sexy	shrinking	sitting still
shaking	shrouded	skeptical
shaky	shrunken	skipped
shame	shy	skipping
shamed	sick	skittish
shamefaced	sickened	slack
shameful	sighing	slaked
shape shifting	sighted	sleep
shaped	silence	sleepy
sharp	silenced	sliced
shattered	silky	slimy
shielded	silly	slippery
shifting	silty	slipping
shining	silver	sloped
shiny	silvery	sloth
shock	simple	slothful
shocked	sinful	slow
shored up	singing	slow moving
shorn	single	sludged up

slurring	sorrowful	squander
small	sotto voce	squandering
smelling	soulful	squat
smelly	space	squeaky
smoky	spacious	squirrely
smooth	spacy	stabbed in the back
smoothed	sparkling	stability
smug	sparkly	stable
sneaky	special	stakeholder
sneezy	speechless	stamped
sniveling	spellbound	standing
snorting	spent	starched
snuffed out	spicy	starchy
soaked	spirited	stargazing
soft	spiritual	starry
sold out	spiteful	startled
somber	spoiled	starved
sonic	spoiled rotten	starving
sonorous	spooky	steady
soothsayer	spreading	steamed
sordid	springy	steamy
sore	spritely	steeled
sorrow	spurned	steely

stellar	stretched	substantiated
sterile	strewn	suffering
sterilized	stringy	sufficient
sticky	stripped	suffocated
stifled	stroked	suffocating
still	strong	sugary
stilted	strung tight	suicidal
stimulated	strung together	sun kissed
stinging	strung up	sunburned
stingy	stubbed	sunny
stinking	stuck	suntanned
stitched together	stumped	supercharged
stoked	stung	superficial
stolen	stunned	supervised
stomped	stunted	support
stopped	stupefied	sure
stopped up	stupid	surprise
stormed	styling	surprised
strangled	stylish	surrounded
strawlike	stylized	suspicious
strength	subdued	sweet
stressed	submission	sweet tooth
stressed out	substantial	swindled

swiveling	**T**	thinking
sympathetic	tagged	thirstiness
sympathy	tan	thirsty
	tanned	thorny
	tanning	thoughtful
	tap	threadbare
	tapped	threatened
	tasteless	thrill
	taught	thrill seeking
	taut	thrilled
	team player	thrilling
	teary	throaty
	teasing	thunderbird
	tender	thwarted
	tenderness	ticking
	tense	tickled
	tensile	tied
	terminated	tight lipped
	terrible	tiled up
	terrified	tilted
	terrorized	tilting
	thankful	time bomb
	thief like	timed

timeless	tranquil	turbulent
timer	transfigured	turmoil
timid	transmuted	turned
timidity	trapped	turning
tinkling	treacherous	twirling
tipsy	trembling	twisted
tired	tremors	tyrannical
to blame	trendy	
tongue tied	tricked	
toothless	trickling	
toothy	trickster	
tormented	trifling	
torn	triumphant	
torqued	troll	
torqued off	troubled	
torqued up	troublemaker	
tortured	troubling	
touch	trust	
touched	trusted	
touching	trusting	
towing the line	trustworthy	
traction	tumult	
traitorous	tumultuous	

U

- unafraid
- unarmed
- unaware
- unbelieving
- uncertain
- uncomfortable
- unconscious
- uncontrollable
- uncooperative
- under a spell
- understanding
- understood
- undiplomatic
- undisciplined
- uneasy
- uneducated
- unfocused
- unfulfilled
- ungrateful
- unhappy
- unholy
- unicorn

- unified
- unifying
- uninterested
- unjust
- unjustified
- unkind
- unloved
- unmannered
- unmovable
- unmoved
- unmoving
- unnerved
- unpleasant
- unprepared
- unprofessional
- unrepentant
- unsettled
- unstable
- unstoppable
- unstuck
- unsure
- untapped
- untouched

- untruthful
- unusable
- unused
- unwilling
- unworthy
- upbeat
- upset
- urge
- urging
- usable
- used
- used up
- useful
- useless

V

vain
valkyrie
valued
vanilla
vanishing
veined
venal
vengeance
vengeful
vertigo
vested
vibrant
victimized
victorious
vigilance
vigilant
vigor
viking
vilified
villainized
vindictive
violent

virginal
visible
visualizing
vociferous
voluminous
voracious
voracity
vulnerable

W

waiting
walled
wallflower
wandering
wanton
war like
warm
warned
warped
warrior
wary
wasted
watchful
watchfulness
water tight
watered down
watery
waxing
wayward
weak
weakness
weary

weather proof	wise	worried
weathered	wishful	worse
weeping	wistful	worsened
weepy	with qualms	wounded
weighted	with source	woven
well defined	withdrawn	wrath
well mannered	withering	wrathful
wet	witty	wretched
whining	wizened	wrinkled
whiny	woe	wrong
white	woeful	wronged
whitened	womanly	wrongful
whitewashed	wonder	wrongly accused
whittled	wonderful	wrung out
whole	wondering	
wholesome	wooden	
wild	wooly	
willful	worked over	
willing	worked up	
willingness	worldly	
wily	wormy	
winded	worn	
windy	worn out	

Y

- yearning
- yellow
- yen
- youthful

Z

- zap
- zapped
- zeal
- zealot
- zealous
- zenith
- zero
- zest
- zesty
- zingers
- zingy
- zipped
- zombie
- zoned out
- zooey
- zoomed in
- zooming

Cycle One: My Feelings

My thoughts are telling me that _____

My body is telling me that

When I listen to all the parts of me, I hear

Understanding My Thoughts

What I've been telling myself about this feeling is _____

What I've learned from listening to my body is

When I ask if those thoughts are really true, I discover _____

My Whole Self

As I listen to my body and know what is true for me, I find that _____

My Next Steps

Now that I have listened to these feelings as messages from my self, to my self, I now choose to_____

_____
_____
_____
_____
_____
_____
_____
_____
_____
_____
_____
_____
_____
_____
_____
_____
_____
_____
_____
_____
_____
_____
_____
_____
_____
_____
_____
_____
_____
_____

The best way for me to take care of my self right now is to _____

Cycle Two: My Feelings

My thoughts are telling me that _____

My body is telling me that

When I listen to all the parts of me, I hear

Understanding My Thoughts

What I've been telling myself about this feeling is _____
_____
_____
_____
_____
_____
_____
_____
_____
_____
_____
_____
_____
_____
_____
_____
_____
_____
_____
_____
_____
_____
_____
_____
_____
_____
_____
_____
_____
_____
_____

What I've learned from listening to my body is _____

When I ask if those thoughts are really true, I discover _____

My Whole Self

As I listen to my body and know what is true for me, I find that _____

My Next Steps

Now that I have listened to these feelings as messages from my self, to my self, I now choose to_____

_____

The best way for me to take care of my self right now is to _____

Cycle Three: My Feelings

My thoughts are telling me that _____

_____

My body is telling me that

When I listen to all the parts of me, I hear

Understanding My Thoughts

What I've been telling myself about this feeling is _____

What I've learned from listening to my body is _____

When I ask if those thoughts are really true, I discover _____

My Whole Self

As I listen to my body and know what is true for me, I find that _____

My Next Steps

Now that I have listened to these feelings as messages from my self, to my self, I now choose to _____

_____
_____
_____
_____
_____
_____
_____
_____
_____
_____
_____
_____
_____
_____
_____
_____
_____
_____
_____
_____
_____
_____
_____
_____
_____
_____
_____

The best way for me to take care of my self right now is to _____

Cycle Four: My Feelings

My thoughts are telling me that _____

My body is telling me that ___

When I listen to all the parts of me, I hear

Understanding My Thoughts

What I've been telling myself about this feeling is _____
_____
_____
_____
_____
_____
_____
_____
_____
_____
_____
_____
_____
_____
_____
_____
_____
_____
_____
_____
_____
_____
_____
_____
_____
_____
_____
_____
_____
_____

What I've learned from listening to my body is _____

When I ask if those thoughts are really true, I discover _____

My Whole Self

As I listen to my body and know what is true for me, I find that _____

My Next Steps

Now that I have listened to these feelings as messages from my self, to my self, I now choose to_____

_____
_____
_____
_____
_____
_____
_____
_____
_____
_____
_____
_____
_____
_____
_____
_____
_____
_____
_____
_____
_____
_____
_____
_____
_____
_____
_____
_____

The best way for me to take care of my self right now is to _____

Cycle Five: My Feelings

My thoughts are telling me that _____

My body is telling me that

When I listen to all the parts of me, I hear

Understanding My Thoughts

What I've been telling myself about this feeling is _____

What I've learned from listening to my body is _____

When I ask if those thoughts are really true, I discover _____

My Whole Self

As I listen to my body and know what is true for me, I find that

My Next Steps

Now that I have listened to these feelings as messages from my self, to my self, I now choose to_____

_____
_____
_____
_____
_____
_____
_____
_____
_____
_____
_____
_____
_____
_____
_____
_____
_____
_____
_____
_____
_____
_____
_____
_____
_____
_____
_____
_____

The best way for me to take care of my self right now is to _____

Cycle Six: My Feelings

My thoughts are telling me that _____

My body is telling me that _____

When I listen to all the parts of me, I hear

Understanding My Thoughts

What I've been telling myself about this feeling is _____

What I've learned from listening to my body is

When I ask if those thoughts are really true, I discover _____

My Whole Self

As I listen to my body and know what is true for me, I find that _____

My Next Steps

Now that I have listened to these feelings as messages from my self, to my self, I now choose to _____

_____
_____
_____
_____
_____
_____
_____
_____
_____
_____
_____
_____
_____
_____
_____
_____
_____
_____
_____
_____
_____
_____
_____
_____
_____
_____
_____
_____
_____
_____

The best way for me to take care of my self right now is to _____

Cycle Seven: My Feelings

My thoughts are telling me that _____

My body is telling me that _____

When I listen to all the parts of me, I hear

Understanding My Thoughts

What I've been telling myself about this feeling is _____
_____
_____
_____
_____
_____
_____
_____
_____
_____
_____
_____
_____
_____
_____
_____
_____
_____
_____
_____
_____
_____
_____
_____
_____
_____
_____
_____
_____
_____
_____

What I've learned from listening to my body is _____

When I ask if those thoughts are really true, I discover _____

My Whole Self

As I listen to my body and know what is true for me, I find that

My Next Steps

Now that I have listened to these feelings as messages from my self, to my self, I now choose to _____

_____
_____
_____
_____
_____
_____
_____
_____
_____
_____
_____
_____
_____
_____
_____
_____
_____
_____
_____
_____
_____
_____
_____
_____
_____
_____

The best way for me to take care of my self right now is to _____

Afterword

If you enjoyed journaling, order a copy of Christina's book <u>Adventure Journaling: A Compass for Self Discovery</u> on Amazon. Several other guided prompt books are available by searching for Christina Dreve on Amazon, or type this link into your browser using this exact link: https://goo.gl/CGTE7s

If you found this helpful, please leave a review wherever you purchased this book. Your review will encourage other people to listen to their feelings too.

You are an important part of bringing and being peace on earth, simply by being you. Thank you for who you are.

About the Author

Christina Dreve coaches aspiring authors to complete their first draft in thirty days. Whether you want to write fiction, non-fiction, memoir, or a business book, Christina can help. Schedule a free project discussion by visiting www.ChristinaDreve.com

www.ingramcontent.com/pod-product-compliance
Lightning Source LLC
Chambersburg PA
CBHW051806100526
44592CB00016B/2581